MW00398428

LAUNCH YOUR CLASSROOM ENGAGEMENT!

FOSTERING A CULTURE OF LEARNING

ANTHONY SCANNELLA
SHARON MCCARTHY

CONTRIBUTORS

Executive Editor - Andrés V. Martín

Developmental Editor - Johnny M. Penley

Lead Copyeditor - Shannon Roberts

Copyeditors - Debra Martín & Katie Hicks

Lead Instructional Designer - Ryan Hennessee

Instructional Designer - Kristina Lunsford & Kyle Pope

Production Manager - Kimberly Daggerhart

Production Editor - Jessica Boyd

Video Production - Johnny M. Penley

Cover Designer - Anna Berger

Book Design and Layout - Andrés V. Martín & Anna Berger

To all the teachers that invited us into their classrooms.

A "no excuses" mentality means that even if you believe it should be students' job to be engaged, you accept that it's your job to engage them.

ERIC JENSEN

CONTENT

PREFACE

WELCOME TO LAUNCH YOUR CLASSROOM!

About the Book

Launch Your Classroom Engagement!: Fostering a Culture of Learning is a book for teachers who want to set up their classrooms for success using fast, powerful techniques that maximize student learning. Inside, you'll find some of the most effective ways to begin the school year and build an environment that encourages student growth. We've transformed years of classroom practice and instructional theory into practical advice you can implement now. From learning about your school to building positive relationships with the people you interact with, *Launch Your Classroom Engagement!: Fostering a Culture of Learning* will help prepare you for some of the most significant challenges in your teaching career.

About the Series

Launch Your Classroom! is a professional development series for educators with a focus on implementation. This is why every professional development book we offer provides a highly visual guide that delivers fast, powerful, and actionable strategies in a way that is easy to understand. Everything we cover is meant to be something that you can use right away. In that spirit, we present you with only the most important information so you can make the biggest impact possible with the limited time and resources you have.

Every *Launch Your Classroom!* book is focused on finding ways to simplify complicated concepts. We use visuals to help make ideas more concrete and videos to further illustrate key concepts. We provide options for different learning styles!

How to Read This Book

We recommend you start by reading the entire book from front to back. Then, as you continue teaching, you can revisit sections as you need them. We also suggest that you keep *Launch Your Classroom Engagement!: Fostering a Culture of Learning* nearby while you're in the classroom so you can reference parts that relate to the skills you're currently developing.

WHAT ARE ROCKET BOOSTERS?

As you progress through each chapter, you'll notice we communicate a lot of information using infographics and Rocket Boosters. Rocket Boosters are blocks of valuable information throughout the book that provide you with further resources about a topic. We divide Rocket Boosters into five categories:

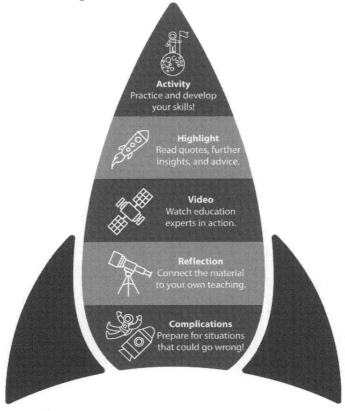

Activity
Practice and develop your skills!

Highlight
Read quotes, further insights, and advice.

Video
Watch education experts in action.

Reflection
Connect the material to your own teaching.

Complications
Prepare for situations that could go wrong!

Important Note: Rocket Boosters have links to our YouTube channel where you can find *Launch Your Classroom!* video resources. All video resources are also available here:

https://www.YouTube.com/EducationalPartnersInternational

PREPARE FOR LAUNCH

INTRODUCTION

Start Here

Whether you're a veteran or rookie, you're sure to have feelings of both fear and excitement about the first day of school. For many teachers, feeling unprepared can be overwhelming. The first day of school is fast approaching, and if you're not ready, your students will know it.

Teachers who've been in the profession for a couple of years can tell you it's never as bad as you imagine. Typically, the pressure you're putting on yourself is a sign of how much you care about doing a great job. Of course, you already know the value of being as prepared as possible—you did pick up this book, after all!

Often, new teachers face a steep learning curve that can directly impact student achievement. We've spent years working with teachers new to the American K-12 classroom. We've worked with teachers of all subjects across all grade levels. As we developed this book, we observed their transition into their classrooms and identified areas where they could benefit from professional development.

As you progress through this book, each chapter will focus on critical strategies to help you deal with the challenges you're most likely to face.

Meet Your Education Experts

We'd like to introduce you to Dr. Anthony Scannella and Sharon McCarthy, educational consultants and authors who've devoted their lives to improving educational systems across the United States of America. They believe in a student-first philosophy and understand how critical the teacher is to providing opportunities for learning. They've helped thousands of teachers develop in their professional capacity.

We look forward to working with you as you launch your classroom engagement this school year, and we hope that you find this book to be an extremely effective resource!

INTRODUCING TONY AND SHARON

Our professional development materials are more than just books. In *Launch Your Classroom!*, you will have access to exclusive video content of your authors and educational experts, Dr. Anthony Scannella and Sharon McCarthy. These videos enhance the material in this book, providing valuable resources, demonstrations, and opportunities for further learning.

To watch this video, please visit:
https://youtu.be/I1H3IWGcD8Y

PART ONE
STUDENT ENGAGEMENT

MOTIVATING AND ENGAGING STUDENTS

Keeping students interested can feel like a huge challenge! In the modern classroom, teachers are competing with endless distractions and shrinking attention spans. How do you reach these students and elicit their involvement in the learning process?

Many teachers incorrectly assume that classroom engagement is limited to managing student attention spans. While developing the skills to command and direct attention is an important first step, engagement is about student investment in their own learning.

An engaged student is curious, self-driven, and excited to discover what happens next. Research has proven that this enthusiasm correlates with success in the classroom.

In this part we're going to cover:

- **Understanding the Neuroscience of Engagement**

- **Getting and Keeping Student Attention**

- **Engaging Students in the Learning Process**

Student engagement isn't about manipulating students into behaving but about creating equal, active, and committed partners in the learning process. A major element in treating students as partners in the learning process involves motivating and convincing them that they can succeed. Throughout this part, we'll share different approaches to help your students feel a sense of accomplishment and a desire to perform.

INTRODUCTION TO STUDENT ENGAGEMENT

Engagement is more than just keeping students on task. In this video, Sharon explains how critically fostering this quality in your classes can be in order to ensure your students are successful.

To watch this video, please visit:
https://youtu.be/yalGlkZ_W0w

ONE
UNDERSTANDING THE
NEUROSCIENCE OF ENGAGEMENT

Educational neuroscience is an emerging field that examines the intersection of the human brain and education. Through the study of how chemical and biological processes are triggered and activated in the brain, educational neuroscience gives us the understanding and the techniques necessary to increase student engagement and learning.

When applying educational neuroscience to your own classroom, there are four main brain chemicals to focus on, each triggered by different techniques:

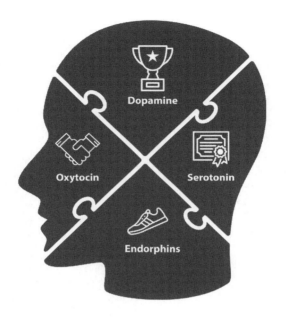

Dopamine - Controls the brain's reward and pleasure centers. Activate it by setting goals and achieving them.

Serotonin - Combats loneliness and depression. Activate it by recognizing achievements and showing gratitude.

Endorphins - Reduces anxiety and depression to help us focus. Activate it through exercise, chocolate, and laughter.

Oxytocin - Controls feelings of trust and promotes bonding. Activate it by doing breathing exercises or listening to soothing music.

By understanding the unique chemistry of the human brain and how it connects to teaching, you can ensure that your students are always in a state of mental readiness that's conducive to learning.

MAKING EDUCATIONAL NEUROSCIENCE WORK FOR YOU

Part of fostering engagement in your students is understanding the mental and biological processes through which engagement happens. In this video, Sharon shares the secrets of marketers and video game designers, walks you through the major neurochemicals that control engagement, and explain what you can do to influence them in the classroom.

To watch this video, please visit:
https://youtu.be/fAkzEjcB71g

STUDENT INTERESTS

At some point, every teacher will hear the question "What does this have to do with me?" or "Why do we have to learn this?" Before you get frustrated, keep in mind: That's a valid question! Students have a difficult time seeing a direct connection to your curriculum and their daily lives. As a teacher, it is part of your job to help them make that connection. When developing your lessons, consider: What are your students' interests? Do they enjoy a particular sport or a specific type of music? How can you insert those interests into your lessons to increase student engagement?

TWO
GETTING AND KEEPING STUDENT ATTENTION

Before you can get your students engaged, you need to grab their attention. There are many ways to accomplish this during instruction. Most of these techniques were defined by researchers Jon Saphier and Robert Gower in their book. *The Skillful Teacher* under the name "Attention Moves."

Attention Moves are actions a teacher can take to capture and keep the focus of students in their classroom (or to get it back once it's lost).

Attention Moves are organized into five different categories: Desisting, Alerting, Enlisting, Acknowledging, and Winning. All have their place in a classroom, and effective instructors will always keep a few in their toolkit. However, to foster a genuine sense of commitment among your students, you should use very few desisting and alerting moves, and more enlisting, acknowledging, and winning moves.

Desisting: These Attention Moves are focused on stopping inappropriate behavior in its tracks. They let the students know that what they're doing isn't acceptable and instruct them to return to the task at hand.

Examples:
Punishment: "You'll need to stay five minutes after class to complete the assignment."
Exclusion: "Since you can't keep your hands to yourself, leave the group and work individually."

Order: "Put your cellphone away, now."

Offer Choice: "Either stop writing that note or read it to all of us."

Proximity: Moving to stand physically close to the student who isn't giving their full attention.

Alerting: Alerting Moves are all about getting students back on task by letting them know you've observed them off task. Rather than direct commands to return to work, these moves keep students in a state of alert anticipation.

Examples:
Using Student Names in Examples: "If Marcello has ten apples and gives two to Gilda, how many does Marcello still have?"

Redirecting Partial Answers: Calling on a student to finish the answer another student is currently giving.

Pre-Alert: "Okay Thomas, what is the answer to number two? Abeer, please be ready if Thomas needs help."

Looking at One, Talking to Another: Looking at a student who isn't paying attention while continuing to speak to another student.

Random Order: Letting students know at the beginning of class that you'll be randomly choosing who answers next, so they can't predict when they'll be called on.

Wait Time: Waiting to speak if a student doesn't immediately know the answer to a question, giving them time to focus and find a response.

Enlisting: Rather than correcting off-task students, Enlisting Moves are about getting interest, investment, and mental buy-in from your class. These moves are based around getting students to choose to participate in instruction and activities.

Examples:
Piquing Student Curiosity: "Now, how do you imagine that this solid piece of ice could become this steam?"

Suspense: "You won't believe how today's history lesson will end! Let's get started."

Challenge: "Now, this one is going to stump everyone I bet."

Student Helpers: "Hester, since you aren't in your seat, maybe you can help me pass out the supplies." Connecting with Student's Imagination: "Pretend we're back in the Cretaceous Period—what dinosaurs do you think we'd be seeing?"

Acknowledging: Acknowledging is a unique Attention Move, because it has only one application: acknowledging out loud to a student your understanding of difficulties they might be facing, in and out of the classroom. This validation can be the spark they need to reinvest their attention in the class.

Examples:
"I understand things aren't the best at home, David. You should know that your fellow students and I are here to support you and your learning."

"Excited about the big game tonight? I bet you're going to do great, just like you will with these word problems."

Winning: The most attractive and the least authoritarian of the Attention Moves are Winning Moves, which are focused on winning students over through your force of personality. These positive moves are all about putting the focus back on the teacher.

Examples:
Encouragement: "You're doing great so far Madeline. Finish strong!"

Enthusiasm: "What a unique answer! That's why I like calling on you, Ang."

Praise: "Outstanding job, Terry. That's something to be proud of."

Humor: Using jokes, not sarcasm, in a way that is positive and enjoyable by students.

SAYING A LOT WITHOUT SAYING ANYTHING AT ALL

How "loud" are your nonverbals? Some of the most important interventions you can execute when inspiring engagement in your classroom aren't words but nonverbal communication. In this video, Sharon provides some tips for developing these techniques.

To watch this video, please visit:
https://youtu.be/AMf2j0oo2ZI

HAND SIGNALS

Verbal Attention Moves can sometimes be the source of a distraction, especially when most students are quietly focused on a task. Other times, your voice can be lost in the crowd of a talkative class. Many teachers find it useful to develop a set of easily interpreted hand signals to use in these circumstances. A good hand signal can get the attention of the student without causing an unnecessary noise or adding to the volume of your room. Hand signals are most effective when they are taught, modeled, then retaught as needed.

NEW TOOLS FOR THE TOOLKIT

Many teachers use some of the same Attention Moves consistently; however, master teachers use different tools for different situations. Teachers who naturally use more authoritarian attention moves can come across as mean or strict. Teachers who exclusively use attractive attention moves can be perceived as not being tough enough.

Set a goal that once a week you'll try one of the moves you don't typically use. This will help you practice your skills and grow your toolkit. You will also engage more students that respond to different attention moves!

REDIRECTION

Our classrooms can be fast-paced and hectic environments, and sometimes the last thing we need in the middle of a lesson or activity is to take time out to get an off-task student back on track.

Instead of wasting valuable class time confronting an off-task student about what they are doing, simply give them a clear reminder of what they should be doing. Rather than focusing on the negative behavior, use redirection to remind them of the correct behavior. This can avoid confrontation and get the student back on task as quickly as possible.

THREE.
ENGAGING STUDENTS IN THE LEARNING PROCESS

When administrators walk past your classroom, they expect to see a class filled with students who are engaged with and invested in their own learning. When students are engaged, they're far more likely to be on task, compliant, and successful.

Successful teachers employ novel and unexpected techniques to introduce learning material, make assignments and activities meaningful, and treat students as active participants in learning rather than passive receptacles.

GREAT STRATEGIES FOR ENGAGING STUDENTS

3-2-1: End each lesson with this activity. After your instruction, students write down three things they learned, two things that were interesting, and one question they have about what they learned that day.

Vote With Your Feet: Incorporating movement in your lessons by having students stand up and move to different locations in the room to voice their position on a topic.

Wired Classroom: Take advantage of student interest in social media by allowing them structured time to post about the current lesson, find images related to the topic, or respond to other students.

Red-Yellow-Green: This technique allows students to have a voice in the lesson and for you to track their progress. At different points throughout the lesson, have students hold up different cards: red indicates a lack of understanding, yellow means a bit of confusion, and green means total understanding.

Ripped from the Headlines: Students respond to material that relates to their lives. Illustrate the relevance of your lesson topic by bringing in newspaper headline clippings, magazine covers, and online media.

FOUR CORNERS

An excellent way to have students "Vote with Your Feet" is using a strategy called Four Corners. Before you begin, you'll need to write the following words, in large print on a piece of poster paper: Strongly Agree, Agree, Disagree, and Strongly Disagree. Place each piece of poster paper in a different corner of your classroom. After the setup, you'll follow this process:

1. Make an opinionated statement related to your curriculum.

2. Have students think about how much they agree or disagree with the statement.

3. Allow the students to move to the corner of the room that best matches their opinion.

4. Call on a variety of students to have them share their rationale out loud.

5. Repeat this process several times with different statements.

This strategy encourages engagement by allowing students to voice their opinions on the material you are learning while increasing their focus through movement. It is particularly useful when introducing a new topic in order to hook your students!

DISENGAGEMENT IS CONTAGIOUS

It may only be a couple of students at first, but disengaged students have a habit of negatively impacting the engagement of other students. If left unchallenged, disengagement will spread throughout your classroom. A positive classroom culture takes participation from everyone, and student disengagement will cause difficulties. Don't wait to tackle engagement problems— you may end up with a much bigger issue than the one you started out with!

ENGAGEMENT THROUGH TECHNOLOGY

As new technologies emerge, so do new challenges with student engagement. Teachers are expected to compete with some very disruptive devices. But, you don't have to see technology as a threat because you can use it as another instructional tool! There are many free-to-download apps made for teachers to use for review, class polling, and even behavior management. In addition, most student devices already have built-in features for learning. Try using the readily available voice recording software to have students practice oral presentations. Make the technology work as an engagement tool for your curriculum!

HELPING STUDENTS WORK BACKWARDS

One of the reasons students may become disengaged from classwork is the complexity or scope of the assignment. For some students, activities performed over a longer period of time can be difficult, abstract concepts.

An effective way to help students overcome this hurdle is to work with them to plan their assignment backwards. Just as instructors begin planning their lessons by contemplating their outcomes and objectives, encourage students to begin planning their project by imagining their final product and working backwards, step by step, from that product.

This process can be easily explained to students through a planning template. For example, it's Monday, and you're giving an assignment that's due Friday. The assignment is to read a specific speech by Abraham Lincoln and another speech from the same time period by Frederick Douglass. You're asking your students to compare and contrast the two leaders' ideas and write an essay on how their philosophies were similar and where they differed.

	Friday	Thursday	Wednesday	Tuesday	Monday
What I Planned For	Turn in Final Draft of Essay	Edit Rough Draft and Create Final Draft	Write the Rough Draft	Organize my Thoughts in a Graphic Organizer	Read the Speeches
What I Actually Did					

Students begin by entering the final product of their assignment onto the square corresponding to the due date. Previous steps are recorded backwards along the template. For example, if a student is required to submit a final draft of an essay on Friday, they might set Thursday as a goal for editing and revising that draft, and Wednesday as a deadline for finishing a rough draft.

Encourage students to reflect on their own actions through this process. How well did they follow their own plan? What would they do differently next time? When they receive their grade, they'll have tangible, visual proof of how they earned the grade they received.

BACKWARDS PLANNING

It can be difficult for learners of all ages to fully understand and execute long-term assignments. In this video, Sharon shares a method of backwards planning that encourages students to begin the assignment with the final product in mind and work back step by step to get there, providing opportunities for teachers to coach along the way.

To watch this video, please visit:
https://youtu.be/MoXJA0DKjPw

THE CLASSROOM OF ENGAGEMENT

What does a classroom that supports student engagement look like? In this video, Tony describes a vision of the Classroom of Engagement and works with a group of educators to define its characteristics.

To watch this video, please visit:
https://youtu.be/W5eYETIMcMw

CONCLUSION

Motivating, encouraging, and above all engaging students is not an easy feat. While many factors outside the classroom impact student performance, teachers play the most important role in fostering engagement. Successful teachers are proactive about engaging their students because this is key to academic, behavioral, and developmental achievement.

Now that you have your students engaged, it's time to put their engagement to the test through student collaboration! Student collaboration and engagement are intertwined. If students aren't engaged, they're unlikely to collaborate effectively with other students. In the next part, we'll discuss how to make the most of partnering your students with one another.

PART TWO
STUDENT COLLABORATION

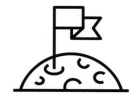

GROUP WORK THAT WORKS

Generations of educational research have proven that learning takes place not only between students and teachers, but also between students and their peers. Many teachers hesitate to incorporate group work into their lesson plans, often with concerns about student productivity or behavior; however creating a collaborative learning environment can be a very rewarding challenge.

Creating a collaborative learning environment that maximizes the effectiveness of student partnership, discussion, and exchange is a rewarding challenge! We'll explore how to make the most out of your student groups through the following topics:

- **Grouping Students for Collaborative Work**

- **Using Effective Structures for Student Collaboration**

- **Keeping Groups on Task**

- **Measuring Learning from Group Activities**

Collaborative activities boost engagement and can create lasting interpersonal relationships. When you group students, you provide them with the opportunity to develop higher-level thinking through communicating with peers. Group work also allows students to become leaders and learn to consider diverse perspectives.

Most importantly, student collaboration teaches students many of the skills they'll be expected to master in the professional world. When students practice their collaborative skills in school, we help set them up for a greater chance of success in whatever career they pursue. Your students have to be ready to work with other people to accomplish common goals!

THE GOOD, THE BAD, AND THE COLLABORATIVE

Many teachers have horror stories about using collaborative group work in their classes, but just as many have exciting stories of how group work was the key to understanding for many of their students. In this video, Sharon works with a group of educators to examine the good and the bad of student collaboration.

To watch this video, please visit:
https://youtu.be/8k_WBlUWafw

THINK-PAIR-SHARE

If you're looking for a place to get started with group work, we recommend the strategy called Think-Pair-Share. This strategy is also known as Turn and Talk.

To help make it easier for you the first time you try the strategy you can use it in a way to allow your students to review the previous unit or lesson. Here's how it works:

1. Give your students a prompt or question related to yesterday's lesson. Then, give them a few minutes to "Think" about their response by themselves and jot it down on some scrap paper.
2. Next, have your students "Pair" up to discuss their responses. During this part of the strategy, you will need to walk around and listen to student conversations. Don't be afraid to support students as they work!
3. Finally, bring the whole class back together to "Share" their answers with the group. Make sure you call on someone from every pair to share.

There are a couple of great things about this strategy. First, it gives students a chance to interact and work together. Some students who might be struggling with their response have an opportunity to hear from one of their peers before being called on. Plus, it's a quick formative assessment. Depending on how your students respond, you can reteach or re-emphasize specific material.

If this is your first time doing this activity with your class, you might not want to let your students choose their partners. The objective for this strategy is to introduce some quick review at the start of the lesson and practice group work. Having students moving around the room to find a partner of their choosing is only going to slow you down and add to the chaos. You can take control of the process by matching up partners by rows or tables.

As you establish rules, guidelines, and routines in your classroom, you can rely on this strategy at any important point in your lesson. This will engage your students to think about what that content means to them and compare their understanding of the material to that of their peers.

FOUR

GROUPING STUDENTS FOR COLLABORATIVE WORK

Once you've decided to implement student collaboration in your classroom, the question arises: how do you group them?

Like everything we do in education, student grouping should be intentional and based on the objective at hand. There are four main methods of grouping students for collaboration: by learning styles, by ability, at random, and student-selected.

SYSTEMS FOR STUDENT GROUPING

Learning Styles: Teachers can group students by a diversity of styles. For example, you may wish to group auditory learners together with visual learners. Groups that contain a mix of learning styles have been shown to learn more from each other and boost the achievement of lower performing students. Rotate the grouping often so students have a chance to learn from others.

Ability: Groups composed of students at the same ability level allows you to provide different degrees of challenge for different groups. Mixed ability groups; however, give the classroom a sense of equality and offer higher achieving students the opportunity to serve as mentors and leaders, while providing lower achieving students with access to the thought process and problem solving of peers they may not otherwise have worked with.

Random: This style of grouping is often seen as the most impartial by students. While it is effective at creating truly diverse groups of mixed abilities and perspectives, there's no guarantee the members of the group will work well together. This type of grouping works best later in the school year after students have learned how to work with one another. To quickly assemble randomized groups, have students count off numbers, draw names from a hat, or use technology.

Student-Selected: Allowing students to choose their own groupings can promote feelings of satisfaction and choice among students. This style of grouping is best used as a reward that students can earn. Teachers should still set guidelines for group composition that impact student success, such as encouraging diversity and separating potential classroom management problems.

Each of the group types listed above have their advantages and disadvantages. Depending on your success, start by grouping students either by learning style or ability before advancing to random and then student-selected. Effective teachers will try different groupings frequently, observe their efficacy, and switch strategies if necessary to best encourage learning in their classrooms.

HOW BIG SHOULD STUDENT COLLABORATIVE GROUPS BE?

The most effective number of students in a group is four or five. Groups of three or less lack the diversity of ideas needed for divergent thinking to occur. Groups of six or larger can become unwieldy, difficult to manage, and provide opportunities for students to "hide" and avoid participation.

GUIDELINES FOR GROUPING

The first question in creating productive and supportive student collaborative groups is the most fundamental: How do you group them? In this video, Sharon shares several methods for grouping your students, and explains when and how to use each to create diverse learning groups.

To watch this video, please visit:
https://youtu.be/wGo5MXWooLo

HOMOGENEOUS OR HETEROGENEOUS GROUPS?

Student group activities can be great for increasing interaction and engagement in your classroom, but you want to make sure that when the time comes to create the groups themselves, you do it intentionally. Your class has many different types of students.

Some may be high achievers, and some may need remediation. Some may be great listeners, and another might be a kinesthetic learner. One student might shine when speaking in front of the class, and this one might rather have others do the talking for them.

So, how do you group them? Well, there's two schools of thought:

- **Homogeneous Groups** - Homogeneous groups place similar learners together and are a great way to differentiate an assignment among different proficiency levels. If you're doing a math assignment and you know that some students are further along in the material than other ones, you can give the more proficient group an assignment appropriate to their academic level. Sometimes these groups might be officially mandated by the school, district, or state, as is the case with reading levels in some elementary grades. Once you get to know your students and their interests, you can occasionally create homogeneous groups based on what they enjoy doing as a class reward.

- **Heterogeneous Groups** - In a heterogeneous group, different types of learners are grouped together. One of the main advantages of a heterogeneous group is the potential for peer mentoring. In a group like this, a struggling student has the opportunity to work with and learn from a higher achieving student. With a mixed group like this, you also don't need to differentiate your assignment. Having students of different achievement levels, learning styles, and interests are also great for creating a positive classroom culture of inclusion.

The critical thing to remember is that there is no right answer for how to create student groups. There are times when a homogeneous group is the best choice, and sometimes a heterogeneous group would be better. Be intentional and choose the group that best fits your classroom objectives.

THERE'S A GROUP FOR THAT

Using the Systems for Student Grouping on the previous page, group your students by each type of system. Really think about each student and how best they learn as you place them into different types of groups. Consider the advantages and disadvantages of each group style. Now, practice using these in your class. What systems do you like most? What systems work best during which type of group activity or subject?

Now pick a system you want to use but which is challenging to implement in your classroom. At the next grade level meeting, ask your colleagues how they effectively use this grouping system. How can you implement their advice in order to use this type of grouping in your classroom?

REMEMBERING GROUPS

Think about two different times in your life when you recall being in a group project - one time when it went poorly and the other time when you feel it was a huge success. Why do you feel those were the outcomes?

Make a chart comparing the reasoning, planning, implementation, and weight of group member responsibility. What do you notice about the group project that went so well? How can you use the same ideas within your classroom to fit the needs and strengths of your students?

ORGANIZING WITH GROUP ACTIVITY FOLDERS

Although very useful, group work can seem a bit chaotic. Students are moving seats, deciding group roles, and collecting materials, while you're reminding them of group specific rules and procedures. There's a lot of potential for lost time and miscommunication. However, you can help to solve these issues by using Group Activity Folders. Insert the following into a folder, such as a three-ring binder, for each group:

• A copy of your group rules, procedures, and norms
• A list of the group roles and their duties
• The group's assignment for the day, including instructions
• Any materials needed to complete the assignment

Make sure to differentiate the group activity folders by colors or labels. Put each group's materials manager in charge of getting the folder once the assignment has begun and returning it with the completed work once the assignment ends!

FIVE

USING EFFECTIVE STRUCTURES FOR STUDENT COLLABORATION

Working in a team doesn't come naturally; even among adults, this skill needs to be taught and practiced. Before you can expect your students to work productively in groups, you'll need to spend time working with your class to develop the structures necessary for group work.

There are two important factors for effective student collaborative groups: roles and norms.

ROLES IN STUDENT COLLABORATION GROUPS

Group roles provide students with explicit expectations, responsibilities, and objectives. When each member of the team has a specific role in the actual project, groups operate more harmoniously and productively.

There are many possible group roles, and depending on the task and group size, not all will necessarily need to be assigned. In addition, students can have more than one role within a group. We've broken down the most common roles on the next page.

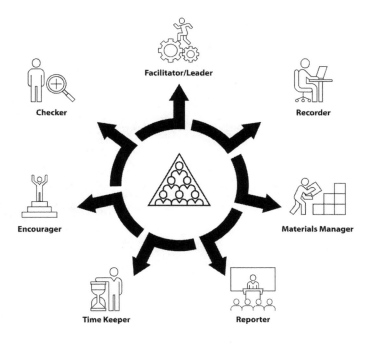

Facilitator/Leader - Keeps the group on task and requires everyone to contribute.

Recorder - Notes important ideas expressed in the group and writes a final summary.

Materials Manager - Collects and distributes materials for the group.

Reporter - Shares summary of group work with the rest of the class.

Time Keeper - Keeps track of time and reminds the group of how much is left.

Encourager - Keeps the group motivated and positive.

Checker - Looks for accuracy and clarity of ideas presented throughout group work.

A ROLE FOR EVERYONE

In an effective learning group, each student has their own role and their own responsibilities. In this video, Sharon describes some of the most common student roles in collaborative groups and provides advice on how to assign them.

To watch this video, please visit:
https://youtu.be/_a84bO3TQc0

THE FACILITATOR

Often, the role with the most responsibility in a student group is that of facilitator. This leadership role helps the group accomplish its goals, keeps everyone on task, and makes sure everyone has a voice. This role can also require the most coaching and instruction from teachers. A successful facilitator:

- Keeps the group on task and on time.
- Manages the group work process.
- Assumes responsibility for the group's progress.
- Encourages productivity and creativity from all participants.
- Alerts teammates when speaking as a facilitator and as a collaborator.

CHANGING GROUP ROLES

One of the goals of a teacher is to prepare students to be well-rounded individuals. If a student fulfills only a single role throughout multiple group activities, they're only learning one way to participate. Have your students change up their group roles periodically so they can gain a better understanding of each group role and its duties. Not only will this help with the student's engagement level, but will also teach them new cooperative skills and give them a sense of respect for their other group members' contributions.

CREATING GROUP NORMS WITH STUDENTS

Groups perform best when all members have a voice in how the group behaves and operates. We call these protocols "group norms": the behavioral standards, traditions, and rules that govern how we function when we work in teams. Without group norms, students won't know how to act when they participate in collaborative groups.

To ensure that students honor and follow group norms, it's important to involve them in the process of creating those norms. This can be a great opportunity to give your students a voice in how the class will run.

CHOOSING NORMS TOGETHER

Partnering with your class to come up with a list of expected group norms is a great way to kick off student collaboration. Early in the school year, before assigning any group activities, work with your students to create group norms on an anchor chart, a visual representation of information that will be prominently posted in the classroom for all to see.

Begin by asking your students to jot down five to seven behaviors that are important to them when working in a group. After having students report back what they've written, work with them to synthesize their lists into a single list by combining similar norms together.

Finally, using a large piece of chart paper, synthesize the list down even further into no more than ten group norms. If students neglect to include important norms like "treating all ideas with respect" or "listening to all voices in the group," this is a good opportunity for the teacher to include them.

GROUP NORMS IN ACTION

Making an anchor chart of group norms with your students is an effective way to create a lasting impression on the productivity and coordination of all future group work in your class. In this video, Sharon explains the importance of group norms and coaches a group of teachers to think like their students as they devise group norm anchor charts.

To watch this video, please visit:
https://youtu.be/N2Y1EmZMVFw

SIX

KEEPING GROUPS ON TASK

One of the main challenges teachers face when implementing collaborative activities in their classrooms is keeping students on task and productive. The main culprit of chaotic classrooms is students' lack of executive function: the system of mental processes that help humans self-regulate, focus, plan, and manage multiple tasks simultaneously.

One method for developing executive function in students is setting goals. When students set their own learning goals and track their progress towards those goals, they increase their own sense of achievement and acquire more effective executive function. Encourage your students to explicitly define how they plan to achieve their goals. This informs students that it isn't just the goal that's important, but also the process.

Fortunately, developing effective student groups and practicing collaborative activities is a tried-and-true method for giving students the opportunity to increase their executive function and self-regulation skills. These processes are important not just for the classroom, but will serve students in their future personal and professional lives.

ENSURE ALL VOICES ARE HEARD

Many beginning teachers dread assigning students collaborative group exercises because they fear students going off task, taking advantage of their teammates' work, and a general sense of disharmony among group members. In this video, Sharon encourages you to make sure all students participate in group work and provides classroom-tested strategies for making sure it happens.

To watch this video, please visit:
https://youtu.be/vFrP7NRg69o

USING STEP SHEETS FOR GROUP WORK

Another way to develop executive function in your students during group work is through the use of Step Sheets. When creating social learning spaces, the more clarity your students have on what to do, how to do it, and how much time each step should take, the more likely your students are to complete the assignment.

Step Sheets break down each step of the collaborative process, both the actual content of the activity as well as the processes of the group itself. An additional benefit of using Step Sheets is that teachers need not repeat instructions over and over; students can simply refer to the sheet.

On the next page is an example of a Step Sheet for a collaborative assignment on the Federal Minimum Wage. The sheet is divided into spaces containing the steps required for the activity, the suggested time for completion of each step, and a section for students to check off when they've completed the step. The curriculum standards that the assignment supports are included at the bottom of the sheet so students can understand the relevance of their work.

Check When Complete	Task	Time
	Determine team roles for this activity: Facilitator, Timekeeper, Recorder, Reporter, Materials Manager, Encourager	2 Minutes
	Facilitator verbalizes the team's norms: all voices heard, respectful communication, everyone works. Team members agree to norms.	1 Minutes
	Team members choose and read the blog post, newspaper, or magazine article about, "Should the federal minimum wage be increased? " It will either be Pro or Con. While reading, team members will identify and highlight three passages that they feel are important to share.	5 Minutes
	Team members take turns reading the first passage they have chosen and state why they feel it is important and factual. The recorder takes notes. This continues until all passages are shared. There will be some duplicates.	5 Minutes
	Team members create an infographic representing their discussion. Post these in an appropriate area.	15 Minutes
	Teams take a walk and review the infographics of the other teams in their class. Any questions are posed to the reporter.	15 Minutes

Common Core State Standards:

CCSS.ELA-LITERACY.RH.9-10.9
Compare and contrast treatments of the same topic in several primary and secondary sources.

CCSS.ELA-LITERACY.RH.9-10.8
Assess the extent to which the reasoning and evidence in a test support the author's claims.

CCSS.ELA-LITERACY.SL.9-10.5
Make strategic use of digital media (e.g., textual, graphical, audio, visual, and interactive elements) in presentations to enhance understanding of findings, reasoning, and evidence and to add interest.

CCSS.ELA-LITERACY.RH.9-10.1.C
Propel conversations by posing and responding to questions that relate the current discussion to broader themes or larger ideas; actively incorporate others into the discussion; and clarify, verify, or challenge ideas and conclusions.

STEP SHEETS FOR SUCCESS

Sometimes a basic learning tool can make all the difference in the classroom. In this video, Sharon discusses the logic behind the simple Step Sheet and how powerful it can be for fostering productivity in collaborative student groups and saving the teacher valuable instructional time.

To watch this video, please visit:
https://youtu.be/6ZOkx30oDtw

SEVEN
MEASURING LEARNING FROM GROUP ACTIVITIES

Often, working in collaborative groups helps students develop interpersonal skills and executive function. Because of this, student reflection and self-assessment on individual and group behavior is important both for their personal development and the efficacy of further group work in your classroom.

Self-assessments given to students should be based around the group norms they created before the assignment. In the example below, students assess both themselves and their group:

Student Collaboration Self Assessment

Your students can use the following key to score how well they carried out each behavior:

I (we) did not do this at all today. - 1 Point
I (we) did this a few times today. - 2 Points
I (we) did this nearly all the time today. - 3 Points
I (we) met this goal completely today. - 4 Points

Behavior	Rating - SELF	Rating - GROUP
I (we) were on task the whole time.		
I (we) respected all voices.		
I (we) listened to all group members' ideas.		
I (we) stayed together; no one went ahead or was left behind.		
I (we) helped the group solve problems.		
I (we) shared our ideas.		
I (we) came to group prepared to work.		
I (we) carried out the responsiblilities of our role.		
	_ / 32	_ / 32

You can add to your quantitative data by collecting some qualitative data with these questions:

1. What tasks did you specifically complete for this project?
2. What do you think was your greatest strength from the list above?
3. What do you think was your weakness that you should work on in your next group project?
4. If you need to defend any of your answers, write comments here:

COLLABORATORS FOR LIFE

One day your students will enter the professional world, and the number one skill employers want to see in prospective employees is the ability to collaborate in groups. In this video, Sharon stresses the importance of creating classrooms of experienced collaborators and demonstrates the use of student evaluations to develop collaborative skills.

To watch this video, please visit:
https://youtu.be/JhneoSM79hs

MANAGING THE FLOW OF CONVERSATION

When students work in collaborative groups, educators sometimes find that students don't know how to manage the flow of their conversation. Luckily, you can help the group's facilitator keep the conversation productive!

A useful way to assist with this process is through Speaking Chips. Using simple plastic chips, students are assigned three talking chips. Each time a student wishes to speak, they must "ante up," so to speak, and put one of their chips into the central pile. When a student is out of chips, they are finished speaking.

Variations on this technique include: systems for students to earn additional Speaking Chips after they have exhausted their own supply and Listening Chips that students must hold up or slide forward when others are speaking.

REVIEWING GROUPS

There are a lot of factors that go into the success of student collaboration. Grouping in your classroom requires thought, planning, continual revisions, and change. Think about the following things:

- How often should you change groups in your class and why?
- How many types of groups should there be?
- How often do you use different group types?
- When thinking about the last time you made groups, did you ever change them?
- If so, was the reason based on data, ability, personality, behavior, or something else?

CONCLUSION

Creating collaborative student groups that are productive, work well together, support social growth, and contribute to a positive classroom environment takes thoughtful planning, careful instruction, and ongoing support. The good news is that many of these skills and dispositions are taught, practiced, and learned while the students are working collaboratively. Encourage your students to work toward becoming a team that functions effectively and efficiently, and it will serve them in their futures.

In some ways, the ability of your class to work together in collaborative groups is a measure of how successful you've been in creating a classroom of cooperative learners.

LIFTOFF!

FOSTERING A CULTURE OF LEARNING

Engaged students are more likely to achieve a high level of academic success due to many factors, but some of the most significant are that they attend class regularly and stay in school. Engaged students are generally less apathetic and contribute to the school community. When students contribute to the school community, they are more likely to promote a safe and positive school culture. This school culture helps students build better relationships with other students, staff, and faculty.

Despite our knowing these facts, in the United States of America, student engagement typically declines as students progress from elementary grades to high school. Some studies estimate that by high school up to 60 percent of students feel disengaged. As professional educators, we have to help our students become more engaged.

Student engagement begins as the responsibility of the teacher. It starts by showing each of your students that you are a caring, involved adult. Every student needs an adult who listens, and you need to be very consistent in how you respond to your students. Understanding the process of how students learn can help you adapt the lesson to meet the needs of all students. You will encounter students who are not intrinsically motivated, so you will need to find different ways to motivate every student. Understanding how your students learn can provide you with insights as to how to help each student learn.

In the best classrooms, students own their learning and support each other. Students do most of the work of driving the engagement level of their peers in these classrooms. To get your class to this point, you have to leverage student collaboration. When students collaborate effectively, engagement is a positive result. Students collaborate by listening, encouraging, and having discussions with their peers.

Student engagement and collaboration are highest when students are entirely respectful with one another while building on their peers' comments, thoughts, and arguments. When your students can transform a discussion, task, or assignment into something more profound than initially planned, you're genuinely fostering a culture of learning.

The difficult task of engaging students in the classroom is one of the most critical aspects of teaching today. When teachers employ effective engagement strategies, they help prevent discipline problems and facilitate classroom management. If a teacher can fully engage every student in their class, they can turn around even the most unruly classrooms.

ABOUT THE AUTHORS

Dr. Anthony Scannella is the former CEO of the Foundation for Educational Administration, as well as an author, psychotherapist, and trainer in the field of neuropsychology. As the founder of The Principal Center for Educational Administration, Dr. Scannella has worked extensively with school administrators from the United States of America and abroad.

Sharon McCarthy is a national educational consultant and author. As president of Envision, Inc., Sharon works with stakeholders at all levels of the school system and has delivered professional development at the state, national, and international levels.

ALSO FROM EDUCATIONAL PARTNERS INTERNATIONAL

To view all of the videos included in this book, please visit our YouTube page:

https://www.YouTube.com/EducationalPartnersInternational

For additional professional development videos and resources, visit our website:

https://teachwithepi.com/professional-development

NOTES

NOTES

_____

_____

_____

_____

_____

_____

_____

_____

_____

_____

_____

_____

_____

_____

NOTES

_____

_____

_____

_____

_____

_____

_____

_____

_____

_____

_____

_____

_____

_____

_____

_____

NOTES

NOTES

NOTES

_____

_____

_____

_____

_____

_____

_____

_____

_____

_____

_____

_____

_____

_____

NOTES

NOTES

NOTES

NOTES

_____

_____

_____

_____

_____

_____

_____

_____

_____

_____

_____

_____

_____

_____

_____

Made in the USA
Columbia, SC
23 June 2019